EXTREME WEATHER

EXTREME WEATHER

ODYSSEYS

MICHAEL E. GOODMAN

CREATIVE EDUCATION · CREATIVE PAPERBACKS

Published by Creative Education and Creative Paperbacks
P.O. Box 227, Mankato, Minnesota 56002
Creative Education and Creative Paperbacks are imprints of
The Creative Company
www.thecreativecompany.us

Design and production by Blue Design (www.bluedes.com)
Art direction by Rita Marshall

Photographs by Alamy (JAH, James Thew), Dreamstime ((c) Artellia), Getty
(Hulton Archive, ISAAC KASAMANI, NurPhoto, Liz Pedersen / EyeEm, Anton
Petrus) iStock (35007, CatLane, Jan-Otto, Pgiam, SeppFriedhuber, Yelantsevv),
Erik Karits, Library of Congress (LOC DSC), NOAA, New Jersey Army National
Guard (Master Sgt. Mark C. Olsen), Sergey Pesterev, Pexels
(GEORGE DESIPRIS, Johannes Plenio), Unsplash (flow clark, Chris
Gallagher, Michael Jin), Wikimedia Commons

Cataloging-in-Publication data is available from the Library of Congress.
ISBN: 978-1-64026-710-7 (library binding)
ISBN: 978-1-68277-266-9 (paperback)
ISBN: 978-1-64000-851-9 (ebook)

LCCN: 2022015455

CONTENTS

Introduction

On October 19, 2012, weather forecasters at the National Hurricane Center in Miami, Florida, noticed a storm gathering in the eastern Atlantic Ocean off the coast of Africa. At first, it was known as "Tropical Depression 18," or the 18th storm of the season. Its wind speed kept increasing as it moved across the Atlantic.

OPPOSITE: The most extreme hurricane-force winds reach more than 150 miles (241 km) per hour, costing people their homes and, sometimes, their lives.

9

On October 22, the storm was officially named Tropical Storm Sandy, the 18th name on that year's alphabetical list. By October 24, the wind speeds reached hurricane level, and the storm became Hurricane Sandy.

At first, Sandy acted like a normal hurricane. It was energized by the warm waters of the Caribbean and tracked northward as it moved toward the United States. Some forecasters hopefully predicted that it would turn east and head harmlessly out into the North Atlantic. But Sandy suddenly changed direction

Hurricane Sandy as seen from space in 2012

on October 28 and began heading west, directly toward New Jersey, and into one of the country's most populous regions. No storm had made such a dramatic turn in 160 years. Meteorologists gave the huge storm a new name—"Superstorm Sandy"—and urged those living along the coast to evacuate inland.

Over the next 10 days, Superstorm Sandy plunged much of the metropolitan New York area into darkness and caused more than $70 billion in damages. Weather scientists began analyzing what had caused Sandy to act the way it did. They also theorized about how changes in Earth's climate might lead to more superstorms and other extreme weather events in the future.

Tracking Trends

Most people start their day by checking the weather. Is it hot, cold, mild, wet, dry, windy, or calm outside? Knowing the weather helps people decide everything from what to wear to what activities to plan—whether to go outside or stay inside. Earth has weather because it is surrounded by a blanket of gases called the atmosphere. The blanket extends about 600 miles (966 km) above and around the surface of Earth.

OPPOSITE: A barometer is a tool to measure the pressure in the atmosphere. Rising high pressure typically means sunny weather, while falling pressure often means wet, windy weather.

As the clouds become denser and heavier, they release some of the water as rain or snow.

The atmosphere provides a filter from the sun's heat that protects the planet from hot or cold temperature extremes that would otherwise make most life impossible. The lowest layer of the atmosphere, about 6 miles (9.7 km) up, is called the troposphere. The troposphere is our weather headquarters. It is filled with swirling gases and **water vapor**, some of which is heated to form clouds. As the clouds become denser and heavier, they release some of the water as rain or snow. Differences in air pressure within the troposphere also result in winds of various speeds that move the clouds.

People have been studying and predicting weather for thousands of years. The Greek philosopher Aristotle (384–322 B.C.) coined the word "meteorology," a term that we still use today, to name the science of weather. Many years later, **Renaissance** scientists developed instruments to measure different elements of weather. In 1593, Italian mathematician Galileo Galilei invented a prototype thermometer used to measure air temperature. His assistant, Evangelista Torricelli, later invented the first barometer to measure air pressure. Galileo's device was never very accurate; German physicist Daniel Gabriel Fahrenheit improved the tool in 1714. Other instruments were soon designed to measure humidity, or moisture in the air. Scientists recognized the need to consider conditions such as temperature, air pressure, and humidity in order to describe and predict weather. Today's meteorologists use sophisticated tools on land, at sea, and in the air to monitor and forecast the weather.

While meteorology has been an area of study for a long time, climatology—the study of climate history and change—is a much newer subject. Weather and climate are closely related, but they have different meanings. Weather consists of short-term changes in the atmosphere—as observed hourly or daily. Climate, on the other hand, explains how

A desert climate is defined by its history of little precipitation.

America's Deadliest Hurricane

On September 8, 1900, a hurricane accompanied by a 16-foot (4.9-m) **storm surge** struck Galveston, Texas, on the Gulf of Mexico. Nearly 20 percent of the city's population of 37,000 died in flooding caused by the storm. It is still ranked as the deadliest hurricane in U.S. history. Galveston was totally unprepared for the storm. When the hurricane was passing over Cuba, the Weather Bureau, based in Washington, D.C., predicted it would move north and east. When the storm turned west, it was too late to warn Galveston residents of the danger coming their way. The 1900 hurricane convinced weather experts to develop a better warning system to help keep people safe.

the weather behaves over relatively long periods, such as decades or centuries. Climatologists usually look at averages in monthly temperature ranges or precipitation over a 30-year period to develop their analyses.

Climatologists first began focusing on climate issues in the mid-1800s. They studied how land areas, oceans, polar ice masses, and winds absorb heat from the sun and move the heat around. They also began observing and collecting data to determine if Earth's climate is changing. They noted that our world has been warming measurably since around 1900. They analyzed the data to determine how this global warming might be affecting the formation and movement of storms that result in extreme weather conditions such as heat waves, floods, and **droughts**.

Nearly all climatologists today believe Earth's climate is undergoing significant changes—most of which are negative. The National Oceanic and Atmospheric Administration, a division of the National Aeronautics and Space Administration (NASA) that focuses on the conditions of the oceans and the atmosphere, has provided the following findings as evidence for this position:

- Earth's average surface temperature has been on the rise since the late 19th century. To measure surface temperature, scientists use readings made by weather stations and buoys above land and ocean surfaces. Then they compare the current readings to those made at intervals in the past. The amount of increase has varied from decade to decade since 1890, but there has been a consistent upward movement. The readings show that most of the warming has occurred in the past 40 years, with the 7 warmest years on record taking place since 2015.

- The oceans have absorbed 90 percent of this increased heat, mostly within the top 2,297 feet (700 m). As of December 2021, the oceans' warmest year on record was 2021.

- The Arctic is warming at twice the rate of the global average. The amount of polar ice that remains in the Arctic at the end of the summer has shrunk by 40 percent since 1979.

- Global **sea level** rose about 8 inches (20 cm) in the last century and has been rising more quickly since 2000. Part of the sea level rise is a result of polar ice melting.

- The number of high-temperature days per year has been increasing. The number of heavy rainfall events per year has also been going up.

Weather Technology

A United Nations agency called the World Meteorological
Organization oversees 11,000 fixed weather stations constructed
in countries around the world. These stations send out reports
every three hours to a group of regional weather centers. The
centers then pass the data to local areas. There are also more
than 1,200 weather stations located on buoys that float freely
with ocean currents and send readings back to land via satellites.
All of these devices keep track of temperature and air pressure
changes, wind speeds and direction, cloud movements, storm
fronts, and precipitation (rainfall and snowfall). In addition,
weather balloons, planes, and satellites take and transmit
photographs that show weather conditions from the air

Current government policies . . . are not enough to curb the extreme effects of global warming.

Climatologists are worried about current trends, and they have published several alarming reports in recent years. One report issued in August 2021 by the United Nation's Intergovernmental Panel on Climate Change (IPCC) issued its starkest warning yet about climate change. The report warned that current government policies to reduce the use of **fossil fuels** are not enough to curb the extreme effects of global warming. Current trends have reached such a critical stage that even if countries take immediate steps, the climate will not start to recover until 2050. Our planet is on course to warm by about 5.4 °F (3 °C), but the IPCC report urges countries to work together to reduce that number to 2.7 °F (1.5 °C) to avoid irreversible changes.

For each additional degree that the global temperature rises, catastrophic weather events will be more frequent. For example, increased global warming could lead to more extremely hot days every summer, which could result in more heat-related deaths and more devastating forest fires. Higher temperatures would also mean more melting of polar ice that could further raise sea levels and flood coastal areas—where much of the world's population lives. A higher rate of global warming could also destroy land and coastal habitats for many animals, ranging from tiny insects that help pollinate crops to huge polar bears.

Countries have a narrow window to stop these climate impacts from getting worse. The IPCC says individuals

can take actions, too. For instance, those who own a home could better insulate the structures, especially around attics, doors, and windows. This could reduce the consumption of energy from fossil fuels. Another energy-saving idea is to install more **solar panels** to generate renewable energy. A third idea involves changing how we get around: Rather than contributing more vehicles to the roads, people could take public transportation where available and walk and cycle more often.

Earth's Greenhouse

Most people agree that Earth's climate is warming. However, not everyone agrees that people are the major cause of climate change. To better understand the issue, it is important to understand just how people and nature interact today and how that relationship is changing the climate.

OPPOSITE: Even in dry areas such as deserts, excessive and prolonged heat can have detrimental effects on the plants and animals in that ecosystem.

There was climate on Earth long before people came on the scene. There was also climate change. There were ice ages—periods of extreme cold in which glaciers covered the land and oceans froze solid. There were also long periods of thawing. Animal and plant life grew and changed during the thawing periods. It is estimated that human life began about 200,000 years ago. Those first humans often faced harsh weather but somehow survived. Earth scientists believe we are in a thawing period now, known as the Holocene, which started about 12,000 years ago. Some scientists refer to the Holocene as the "age of people" because the human population on Earth has grown so rapidly during this time—from about 5 million to more than 7.9 billion in 2022.

One main reason that humans have flourished during the Holocene is that temperatures have been fairly warm and steady throughout the period. Earth is heated naturally by a process known as the "greenhouse effect." Light from the sun enters Earth's atmosphere and warms the ground and oceans, much like light enters a greenhouse and warms plants inside. Some of the sun's heat bounces back in the form of infrared rays. These rays are kept from escaping back into space when they are absorbed by gases in the atmosphere, especially carbon dioxide (CO_2). The greenhouse effect involves a delicate balance. Climatologists worry that human activity, particularly in the past 250 years, may be destroying that balance.

More prolonged periods of heat and drought
brought on by climate change make trees
and other vegetation more susceptible to wildfires.

What has been significantly different about climate change in the distant past and climate change recently is the industrialization that began in the 1700s. To generate power to run machines in factories and homes, to propel vehicles, or to heat and cool buildings, people began burning more and more fossil fuels, such as coal, oil, and gas. One byproduct of fossil fuel burning is an increase of CO_2 in the atmosphere. Some CO_2 is vital. Without enough heat-trapping CO_2, Earth's temperature would be too cold to sustain human life. With too much CO_2, however, our atmosphere might overheat. That seems to be going on today. Based on measurements that climatologists have been taking since around 1850, Earth has gotten about 1.3 °F (0.72 °C) warmer on average. And the average temperature increase is expected to go up even faster in the future. If the temperature in your home goes up less than a degree, you may not notice the change very much. However, if the whole planet heats up even a small amount, there can be major consequences for all life-forms.

That is what meteorologists thought was happening in 1988. It was a turning point for weather scientists. In 1988, U.S. weather did not follow normal climate patterns. Spring temperatures were above normal, summer temperatures were sweltering, and fall temperatures remained extremely high. In May, record highs were recorded in 13 cities. In June, another 69 cities set heat records. In July, the temperature in normally moderate San Francisco, California, hit 103 °F (39 °C). Los Angeles topped that record with a 110 °F (43 °C) reading in September. People were not the only ones suffering. Farmers in North Carolina reported that the severe heat wave resulted in the deaths of 166,000 chickens and 15,000 turkeys.

The weather was not only hot in 1988, it was also very dry. The Midwest experienced one of the worst droughts ever. Without rain, crops withered, and farmland dried up. The water level in rivers and lakes also fell. It was inevitable that heat and dryness would lead to fires breaking out. That is what happened in Yellowstone National Park, where 36 percent of the trees and other vegetation were destroyed by fire in the summer of 1988.

Paris Agreement

At the United Nations Framework Convention on Climate Change in Paris, France, in 2015, most of the world's nations signed an agreement to increase use of green energy sources, reduce use of fossil fuels, and take other measures to limit global warming. The agreement is known as the Paris Climate Accord. The signees agreed to submit plans detailing what actions their countries would take to help meet specific global warming reduction goals. They also agreed to pledge money to help implement the pact. The agreement's ultimate goal is for its members to reach net-zero emissions by 2050.

U.S. government leaders wondered if all of these weather events could be interrelated. A senate committee invited James Hansen, director of NASA's Goddard Institute for Space Studies, to explain what was happening. Hansen presented studies that linked the record heat and drought to the greenhouse effect and to human activity. He urged leaders in the U.S. and around the world to begin taking steps as soon as possible to deal with climate change. Hansen's remarks helped prompt the United Nations to form the IPCC. The panel has been assessing scientific studies related to climate change ever since, publishing reports on the findings every five to seven years.

While Hansen focused his attention on the impact of global warming on land, other NASA scientists

Warmer oceans and warmer air above the oceans result in a perfect "breeding ground" for severe storms such as hurricanes.

looked for connections between global warming and storm activities taking place over Earth's oceans. They noted that readings from buoys and satellites showed that surface temperatures of ocean waters have been increasing since the 1970s. So has the temperature of air above the oceans. Because warm air holds more water vapor than cold air, rising air temperatures have led to an increase in the amount of water vapor in the atmosphere. Warmer oceans and warmer air above the oceans result in a perfect "breeding ground" for severe storms such as hurricanes. These storms require high humidity, strong winds, and surface ocean temperatures that exceed 79 °F (26 °C). The rising of warm, moist air from the ocean combines with water vapor already in the atmosphere to feed the storm. So, it might seem logical that global warming has led to an increase in the number and intensity of hurricanes. Recent statistics support this conclusion.

Between 1969 and 1999, in the North Atlantic Basin (an area encompassing the Caribbean and parts of North America), there were an average of 11 named tropical storms each year. A named tropical storm is promoted to hurricane level when its winds reach 74 miles (119 km) per hour. Approximately 6 of those 11 reached hurricane level each of those years. More recently, the average season has 12 named tropical storms and 9 hurricanes. Of the last 26 seasons, 18 have been above

Names and No Names

Since 1953, Atlantic hurricanes have been given names from alphabetical lists compiled by the National Hurricane Center. One name is assigned each year for 21 letters (all except *Q, U, X, Y, and Z*). The names are reused every six years. However, the names of especially deadly or costly storms have been retired forever, such as Katrina, Sandy, Harvey, Michael, and Laura. They are replaced on the list by other names. In 2020 and 2021, there were so many big storms that the NHC ran out of names and began using letters of the Greek alphabet.

normal. The 2021 Atlantic hurricane season was the third most active on record with 21 named storms, 7 of which were hurricanes. The increase in activity is likely due to a seasonally warm phase of sea surface temperature that started in 1995 and lasts 20 to 40 years. However, the IPCC reports that a greater number of storms are becoming hurricanes due to global warming. Scientists believe the combination of warmer waters and warmer air above those waters are leading to larger, stronger, and longer-lasting storms.

Hurricanes Jose *(top left)* and Maria *(bottom right)* as seen from space in 2017

A number of these devastating storms made landfall in the U.S. in the 2000s. Hurricane Katrina, which struck the Gulf Coast near New Orleans, Louisiana, in 2005, is one of the deadliest and most costly hurricanes in U.S. history. More than 1,800 people died as a result of Katrina. Damages from the storm were estimated at $160 billion. It took parts of the New York and New Jersey coasts years to recover after Superstorm Sandy hit in 2012. Slow-moving Hurricane Harvey drenched the Houston, Texas, area with more than 60 inches (152 cm) of rain over a 4-day period in August 2017. Later that same year, Hurricane Maria destroyed much of the island of Puerto Rico. In 2021, Hurricane Ida made landfall in Louisiana and was almost as intense as Hurricane Katrina. It caused $64.5 billion in damages.

Going to the Extreme

Think about the weather events you or your family members have experienced in your lives. Have you ever been drenched or buffeted by a hurricane or taken shelter from a tornado? What is the hottest day you have sweated through or the coldest day you have shivered through? The most consecutive days of rain or the longest period of drought?

Hurricanes, tornadoes, flash floods, extreme heat, wildfires, tsunamis, severe thunderstorms, mudslides, snow and ice storms . . . the list can seem pretty scary. Luckily, not every part of Earth experiences all of these extremes. There is some concern, however, that global warming may be causing extreme weather events to occur more frequently and with greater impact. For example, much of the planet is experiencing heat waves of greater frequency and intensity than in the past. These present a very real danger. According to a report issued by the National Weather Service, more people on average die of heat-related causes each year than as a result of hurricanes, tornadoes, floods, or lightning.

Hurricane activity is also increasing today. The increase is not so much in the number of storms but in

THE SAFFIR-SIMPSON HURRICANE SCALE

CATEGORY	WINDS		DAMAGES
	(mph)	(km/h)	
1	**74 - 95**	**119 - 153**	Very dangerous winds Some damage
2	**96 - 110**	**154 - 177**	Extremely dangerous winds Extensive damage
3	**111 - 130**	**178 - 209**	Devastating damage
4	**131 - 155**	**210 - 249**	Catastrophic damage
5	**> 156**	**> 250**	Catastrophic damage

their strength or size. Hurricanes are given a category ranking of 1 to 5, based on the strength of their sustained winds. The Saffir-Simpson Scale was developed by wind engineer Herbert Saffir and meteorologist Robert

Simpson in the 1970s as a tool for alerting the public about the possible impact of hurricanes. It describes the characteristics of each category.

Based on a NASA analysis of global hurricane data, the number of storms per year that are rated Category 2 or Category 3 has increased significantly since 1980. Storms are sustaining hurricane wind speeds for longer periods of time after they first make landfall. Some of today's storms are also moving more slowly than in previous times, and there is a greater chance that they will drop record amounts of rain.

Category ranking is one way that meteorologists measure the power and destructiveness of hurricanes. But sometimes a new way is needed. That's what happened with Hurricane Sandy in 2012. Sandy began as a Category 1 storm when it entered the Caribbean region. Then its winds sped up between Jamaica and Cuba, and it was elevated to Category 2. As it traveled in the Atlantic Ocean between Florida and Virginia, Sandy was back to a Category 1. Then something unusual occurred. As Sandy was seemingly ready to head safely eastward out to sea, it ran into a cold front coming down from Canada, which changed its wind patterns. Sandy turned to the west and began heading toward New Jersey. Its winds were strengthened by the combination of storm fronts, and its overall size was expanded. It became so huge and dangerous that weather forecasters decided to

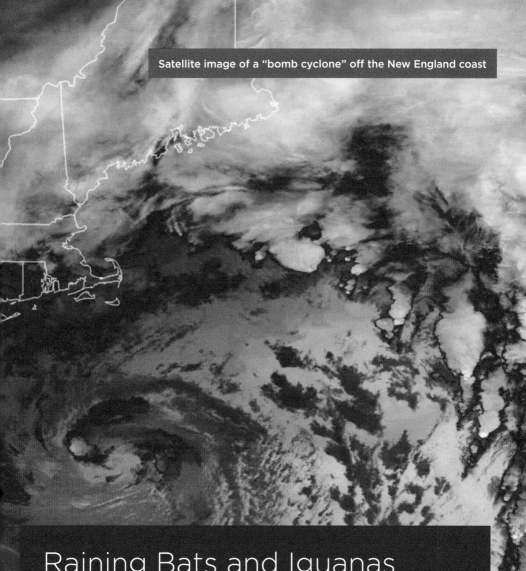

Satellite image of a "bomb cyclone" off the New England coast

Raining Bats and Iguanas

Extreme changes in climate are affecting many animal species. In southeastern Australia, where temperatures in 2018 reached more than 110 °F (43 °C), several hundred large bats—gray-headed flying foxes— dropped from the sky, killed by the heat. In contrast, in South Florida, where temperatures were much colder than usual, numerous iguanas fell from trees, temporarily frozen. When temperatures warmed up days later, some of the iguanas recovered. Sharks in the waters near Cape Cod in Massachusetts were not as lucky as the iguanas. After a severe cold front called a "bomb cyclone" struck in March 2018, many thresher sharks washed up on the beach, frozen to death.

call it a "superstorm." Meteorologists believe that many more superstorms will occur in the future as a result of global warming.

Hurricanes are not the only types of extreme weather events that are intensifying in the 21st century. Perhaps the most deadly events are tsunamis, which typically occur in the Pacific or Indian Oceans. "Tsunami" is a Japanese word meaning "harbor wave." Tsunamis usually follow earthquakes that shift land and open areas along the seafloor. The ocean waters move in to fill the gap. Then the waters are pushed outward as a series of giant, fast-moving waves. The waves, which can reach speeds of nearly 500 miles (805 km) per hour, often overflow anything in their path as they hit the shore.

One of the world's most powerful tsunamis occurred the day after Christmas in 2004. It began with a major earthquake centered near Indonesia. That set off giant waves that rushed ashore throughout southern Asia. In all, 230,000 people in 14 different countries died as a result. The tsunami became one of the deadliest natural disasters ever recorded.

Extreme weather is not something new, though. The world has been experiencing extreme weather events for hundreds of years. Some we know about; others were probably never written or talked about. Here are a few of the most memorable weather events of the past:

- On May 19, 1780, most of New England experienced nighttime darkness in the middle of the day. Many religious New Englanders believed the world was ending. The cause of the darkness was later determined to be heavy cloud cover combined with thick smoke from nearby forest fires.

- The year 1816 became known as the "Year Without a Summer." Temperatures stayed far below normal all summer long throughout the U.S., Canada, and western Europe. A heavy snow fell in New England in June. Many parts of the world—including China and India— experienced extreme rains and droughts, and farmers worldwide lost most of their crops.

What had caused the extreme summer chill? The eruption of a volcano in Indonesia in April 1815 had sent tons of ash and poisonous gases into the air, where they remained for a long time. The ash reduced the heat and light of the sun, affecting the entire Northern Hemisphere.

- Cyclones are hurricanes that form over the South Pacific and Indian Oceans. They can be particularly destructive in the Bay of Bengal in northeastern India. One cyclone in October 1864 created a 40-foot (12-m) wall of water that flooded the entire city of Calcutta, India. More than 60,000 people were killed during the storm. Many thousands more died later from disease.

- In the Australian summer from October 1923 to April 1924, parts of western Australia experienced a world heat-wave record when the temperature topped 100 °F (38 °C) for 160 consecutive days.

Extreme weather has even influenced wars in history. In 1415, heavy rains and deep mud helped the English defeat the French in the decisive Battle of Agincourt during the Hundred Years' War (1337–1453). In 1588, when the ships of the Spanish Armada were sailing into English waters, strong winds stalled the invading ships and helped the English sink much of the Spanish fleet. A destructive hurricane in the Caribbean in 1780 sank many British ships that might have been used to fight the Continental forces during

the American Revolution (1775–1783). Bitterly cold Russian winters also played a key role in the defeat of both Napoleon's French army in 1812 and Adolf Hitler's German army in 1942.

EMERGENCY

CANDLES

ST AID KIT

TCHES

DISASTER PREPARATION LI

- WATER
- NON-PERISHABLE FOOD
- BATTERY RADIO
- BATTERIES
- FIRST AID KIT
- FLASHLIGHT
- BLANKET
- CANDLES
- CAN OPENER
- PRESCRIPTION MEDS
- PET FOOD

- CELL PHONE
- MATCHES
- WHISTLE
- CASH & KEYS
- HAND SANITIZ
- BASIC TOOL S
- TRASH BAGS
- BABY SUPPLIE
- EMERGENCY C
- PERSONAL HY
- DUST MASK

Survival Planning

Extreme weather events seem to be happening more frequently in current times. Heat waves and snowstorms, flash floods and droughts, mudslides and wildfires are constantly in the news. In the year 2021 alone, there were 18 weather disasters in the U.S. A megadrought in the West lasted for most of the year, leading to water shortages and huge wildfires.

OPPOSITE: Every home should keep and maintain a disaster supply kit that includes water, non-perishable food, a first aid kit, and other basic survival items.

A winter storm in February 2021 brought snow and ice to areas as far south as Texas, causing widespread power outages to 10 million people. It was the costliest winter storm in the U.S., with $20.8 billion in damages. In April, hail the size of baseballs fell during storms in Texas and Oklahoma. A heat dome settled over the Pacific Northwest, shattering high temperature records in June. Tropical Storm Fred, Hurricane Ida, and Hurricane Nicholas hit the Atlantic coast in August and September. Hawaii saw its lowest temperatures in 60 years, with a blizzard blowing atop its mountains, in early December. Meanwhile, a heat wave was hitting the Midwest. Cities in Iowa, Kansas, and Missouri all felt record high temperatures in the 70s on December 15. And a tornado outburst ripped through eight states in the central and southern U.S. in December, too.

Costly Disasters

Not only are extreme weather events hazardous, they are also very expensive. Damaged homes, businesses, vehicles, crops, and livestock all add up. From From 2017 to 2021, there were $742 billion in damages in the U.S. Data from these years shows that losses from hurricanes and wildfires have grown in the past decades, indicating that the strength of these weather events has increased. Hurricanes are stronger due to warming temperatures. Wildfires spark easier and spread faster due to dry conditions from heat waves and droughts. The 2020 wildfires in the western U.S. burned a record-setting 10.2 million acres (4.1 million ha)—almost double the size of New Jersey—and cost $16.5 billion from burned structures and smoke damage.

On foot, bundled up, is often the only option for getting around in a heavy snowstorm.

t is quite possible that you will come face-to-face with an extreme weather event in your life. Suppose the weather forecast where you live calls for a hurricane, tornado, flooding rains, a heat wave, or a blinding snowstorm. Would you know what to do to keep yourself and your family safe? Meteorologists and emergency management experts have both been focusing on the best ways to survive weather emergencies. Numerous books and websites are available with advice. At the core of it all is the need to develop a family disaster plan and to create a personal emergency supply kit. The American Red Cross has published step-by-step emergency plans.

The Red Cross says any family plan should have three parts: (1) Family or household members should discuss how to prepare and respond to the types of emergencies

that are most likely to happen where they live, learn, work, and play. (2) They should identify responsibilities for each member of the household so that they work together as a team. (3) They should practice as many elements of the plan as possible ahead of time. The family plan should also cover what to do if members get separated. In that case, two meeting places should be chosen—one nearby and another outside the neighborhood, if it is not safe to stay near home. A disaster supply kit can be just as vital as an emergency plan. See the Red Cross's website for a list.

Each type of weather disaster poses its own problems. For example, preparing for a hurricane means securing roofs and boarding up windows to prevent glass from breaking and endangering people inside the home. It is a good idea to clear any rain gutters of debris that might clog them in a heavy rain. Disinfect the bathtub and fill it with water for bathing or for flushing toilets in case the home water supply gets cut off.

Tornado safety calls for different preparation. First, you need to decide whether to evacuate your home and go to a public shelter or stay home and wait out the tornado. The choice may be determined by the amount of time available before the tornado hits. If you stay home, get away from windows and outside walls. Seek the lowest and most central part of the home or go into a bathroom,

NORTH LOSEY,
View Photographer.

OKLAHOMA CITY,
Okla.

Flash flooding can occur when a large amount of rain falls within a very short period of time. In urban areas, the water overwhelms drainage systems and quickly floods the streets.

Flash floods are particularly dangerous, whether you are caught while riding in a car or while walking.

where the walls are usually reinforced by water pipes. Try to get under a mattress or cover yourself with blankets to help protect against blowing debris. After a tornado passes, the most important thing is to check your own safety and then to see if others need help.

Flash floods are particularly dangerous, whether you are caught while riding in a car or while walking. If in a car, the best advice is to turn around and not drive through the water. It is hard to judge just how deep the water is. If the car is stuck, power down the windows before the car's electrical system shorts out. You may need to escape through a window. If you abandon the vehicle, make sure you have a clear path to higher ground. If not, it may be best to climb on the car's roof and wait for help.

In case of a heat wave, some important tips include these precautions: Avoid strenuous activity. Dress for summer in lightweight, light-colored clothing. Cut down on protein consumption, which can increase body heat. Drink plenty of water and limit caffeinated beverages. Never leave children or pets alone inside a car, even with the windows down.

What do experts suggest doing if someone is caught in a car in a heavy snowstorm? First of all, it is best to stay put unless a building is nearby. Make sure the exhaust pipe is clear of snow, so **carbon monoxide** will not build up. Turn the car off to conserve gas but turn it on for short periods of time to let the heater warm you up. Keep your hazard lights on, both to alert rescuers and to make sure other cars don't run into yours.

Emergency planning will become more and more important as Earth's air and waters continue to undergo warming. It is vital that government leaders around the world focus on how best to deal with climate change and how best to help people prepare for extreme weather events. The time to act is now.

LOST DOG

REWARD REWARD

last seen near 71st Avenue and Union Turnpike, Forest Hills

He is a small black and gray poodle wearing a black and orange harness with a black leash. He goes by the name of Shadow and is frightened very easily.

Pet Emergency Plan

When people with pets are forced to evacuate their homes in a weather emergency, what should they do with their pets? Of course, it would be best to take their pets with them. However, not all shelters, hotels, or motels will accept pets. So it is important to determine before an emergency which places to go with pets or the best places to leave pets. Veterinarians recommend microchipping pets as a permanent form of identification. Owners should also carry recent pictures of their pets with them in case they become separated from the pets and need to make a "lost" poster.

Selected Bibliography

Barnett, Jonathan, and Matthijs Bouw. *Managing the Climate Crisis: Designing and Building for Floods, Heat, Drought, and Wildfire*. Washington, D.C.: Island Press, 2022.

Climate Central. *Global Weirdness: Severe Storms, Deadly Heat Waves, Relentless Drought, Rising Seas, and the Weather of the Future*. New York City, N.Y.: Pantheon Books, 2012.

Cunningham, Anne C., and Kenneth Green. *Climate Change: A Threat to All Life on Earth*. New York City, N.Y.: Enslow, 2016.

Curley, Michael. *The Price of Climate Change: Sustainable Financial Mechanisms*. Boca Raton, Fla.: CRC Press, 2022.

Fleischer, Jeff. *A Hot Mess: How the Climate Crisis Is Changing Our World*. Minneapolis, Minn.: Zest Books, 2021.

Intergovernmental Panel on Climate Change. "Special Report: Global Warming of 1.5 °C." https://www.ipcc.ch/sr15/.

Letcher, Trevor. *Climate Change: Observed Impacts on Planet Earth*. Cambridge, Mass.: Elsevier, 2021.

Sobel, Adam. *Storm Surge: Hurricane Sandy, Our Changing Climate, and Extreme Weather of the Past and Future*. New York City, N.Y.: HarperCollins, 2014.

Glossary

carbon monoxide a colorless, odorless gas that can be deadly if too much is breathed in

drought a long period of dry weather in which crops fail and farmland dries up

fossil fuel a natural fuel, such as coal, oil, or gas, formed in the geological past from the remains of living organisms; burning fossil fuels gives off carbon dioxide, which may contribute to global warming

glacier a large mass of ice formed over a long period of time from the packing and freezing of snow

green energy energy that comes from natural, renewable sources such as sunlight, wind, rushing water, and plants

hurricane level storm strength in which wind speeds exceed 74 miles (119 km) per hour

industrialization a period in which people began to use machines powered by fossil fuel sources to do work

landfall when a tropical storm leaves the ocean and encounters land

Renaissance	the historical period in Europe between the 14th and 17th centuries when there was a renewed interest in art, literature, and science
sea level	the level of the sea's surface in relation to shorelines
solar panel	a device designed to absorb the sun's rays to generate electricity or heat
Spanish Armada	a fleet of warships sent by Spain to attack England in 1588
storm surge	a rising of the sea, pushed by air pressure changes, tides, and strong winds; it often causes flooding
tsunami	a high, powerful sea wave, often caused by an earthquake, that can cause great damage and drown many people when it comes ashore
water vapor	the gaseous form of water in the air

Websites

NASA: Global Climate Change
https://climate.nasa.gov
This site provides up-to-date articles and resources on climate
    change.

National Oceanic and Atmospheric Administration
https://www.noaa.gov/
Learn about the conditions of the oceans, major waterways,
    and the atmosphere.

NOAA: U.S. Billion-Dollar Weather and Climate Disasters (2022)
https://www.ncdc.noaa.gov/billions/
This site has up-to-date figures on the latest billion-dollar
    disasters in the U.S.

Red Cross: Preparedness Guide—"Be Red Cross Ready"
https://www.redcross.org/content/dam/redcross/local/
    NCCR/148816preparednessguide_web.pdf
Read how to be prepared and what to do if extreme weather
    affects your home.

Index